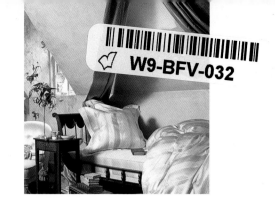

GLOUCESTER MASSACHUSETTS

Comfort COLORS

PALETTES FOR LIVEABLE ROOMS

ROCKPORT PUBLISHERS

by Melanie and John Aves

First published in the United States of America by:
Rockport Publishers, Inc.
33 Commercial Street
Gloucester, Massachusetts 01930-5089
Telephone: (978) 282-9590
Facsimile: (978) 283-2742

Distributed to the book trade and art trade in the United States by:
North Light Books, an imprint of
F & W Publications
1507 Dana Avenue
Cincinnati, Ohio 45207
Telephone: (800) 289-0963

Other Distribution by:
Rockport Publishers, Inc.
Gloucester, Massachusetts 01930-5089

ISBN 1-56496-464-7

10 9 8 7 6 5 4 3 2 1

Designer: Evelyn C. Shapiro
Design assistance and production: Jeanne L. McCready
Cover Image: Anthony Antine, Antine Associates, Inc.

Printed in Hong Kong.

Design: Al Evans

Acknowledgments

COMFORT COLORS has been a pleasure to bring from idea to reality, because of interest, support, and encouragement from many outstanding professional designers from all across the United States. A large group responded to our survey, and their thoughtful answers helped us give a more accurate description of the effects color has on our feelings inside a space. We are confident that these designers, who have direct experience working with color in many situations on a regular basis, are the best authorities available on this subject. The designers who enthusiastically responded to our survey are:

Diane Alpern Kovacs, *Diane Alpern Kovacs Interior Design, Inc.*
Anthony Antine, *Antine Associates, Inc.*
Brett Beldock, *Brett Design, Inc.*
John Berenson, *John Berenson Interior Design*
Patricia Bonis, *Patricia Bonis Interiors, Inc.*
Ronald Bricke, *Ronald Bricke & Associates, Inc.*
Mary Delany, *Mary Delany Interior Design*
Al Dickerson, *Klingman's of Grand Rapids*
Donna Dunn, *Donna Dunn & Associates*
Barbara Eberlein, *Eberlein Design Consultants, Ltd.*
William R. Eubanks, *William R. Eubanks Interior Design, Inc.*
Al Evans, *Al Evans Interiors*
Paula Fogarty, *Kindel Furniture Company*
Gary Gibson, *Gary Gibson Interior Design*
Phyllis G. Goldberg, *PGG Interiors*
Steven M. Hefner, *Designworks Creative Partnership, Ltd.*
Allison A. Holland, *Creative Decorating*
James R. Irving
Stacey Lapuk, *Stacey Lapuk Interior Design, Inc.*
Vince Lattuca, *Visconti + Company*
Lise Lawson, *Lise Lawson Interior Design*
Susie Leader, *Susie Leader Interiors*
Ellen Lemer Korney, *Ellen Lemer Korney Associates*

Lila Levinson, *Accent on Design*
Susan Lovelace, *Lovelace Interiors*
Sandra Nunnerley, *Sandra Nunnerley, Inc.*
Gayle Reynolds, *Gayle Reynolds Design*
Justine Ringlien
Lynn Robinson, *Lynn Robinson Interiors*
Pedro Rodriguez, *Pedro Rodriguez Interiors*
David A. Seglin, *HSP/Ltd., Seglin Associates*
Gail Shields-Miller, *Shields & Company Interiors*
Ho Sang Shin, *Antine Associates, Inc.*
John Staff, *J. Staff Architect*
Pat Stotler, *Pat Stotler Interiors*
Anne Tarasoff, *Anne Tarasoff Interiors*
Stanford R. Thigpen, *Stanford R. Thigpen Interiors, Inc.*
Jean Valente, *Jean Valente, Inc.*
Jill Vantosh, *Vantosh & Associates*
Stephanie Walters, *Parisi Interior Design*
Carole Weaks, *C. Weaks Interiors, Inc.*
Sue Wenk, *Sue Wenk Interior Design*

We also appreciate the fact that we could not show our readers such a comprehensive selection of the finest examples of contemporary interior design without the excellent photography many designers have contributed to our project. Photographing interiors is a highly specialized process, and we are fortunate to have the work of many of the most exceptionally talented photographers in the field represented here.

We especially acknowledge our daughter, Alison Aves, for her meticulous work in setting up our files and managing the beginning of our project. We also acknowledge Bethany Lacina for her assistance in tabulating our research. And finally, Jennifer Ruiter and Jeanine Caunt provided invaluable assistance in the completeion of this project.■

Contents

Design: Paula Fogarty

Design: (above) Gayle Reynolds, (opposite page, top to bottom) John Berenson, Gary Gibson, Mary Delaney

Preface

WE HAVE TALKED WITH MANY DESIGNERS and other readers since our first book on color in interior design was published in 1994. The questions that most often kept discussions lively were about the effects of color on mood. Recent interest in the West about the Eastern tradition of Feng Shui reflects our curiosity about the effects of the outer world on our inner spiritual worlds. We decided to ask professional designers to share their insights about color and comfort based on years of experience working with clients from all over the country, clients with different backgrounds, style preferences, and budgets.

In this book we will show how these designers use the power of color to elicit a particular emotional response or mood in a room, how they manage color to create comfortable places to eat, rest, work, and play. We will share some of the research on the effects of specific colors on our psyches, and we will show effective color combinations created by experts in a variety of rooms which serve different human needs. The decorating styles featured are diverse, but all are inspired. We will show what colors designers prefer for different spaces in the home so that the reader may gain confidence to experiment with original color combinations to suit personal needs and preferences. ■

CHAPTER ONE

Color and Our Sense of Well-Being

———◆◆◆———

Color has a profound effect on the way we feel in a space. Each person has a different response to color based on his or her life experience and genetic predisposition. It follows that generalized interior design guidelines about what colors to use where are often inappropriate and unnatural.

Color is significant and mysterious. It has impact on human beings symbolically, historically, and psychologically. The human emotional response to color may be explained in terms of both instinct and conditioning. For ancient peoples the sun was the ultimate source of light and color. In modern times, the effects of light upon humans and the electromagnetic energy light produces fascinate us and continue to be studied. We have learned more about the physical properties of color, and yet our explanations of its psychological properties are at best incomplete.

Light, and therefore color, are also essential to a healthy physical existence. The rhythm of light has a powerful effect on the human body; the absence of light can even produce a state of seeming hibernation. Newborn babies need exposure to light to maintain good health and normal growth patterns, but prolonged exposure can cause health problems as well. The most confounding aspect of research in this area is that because the effects of light and color are transient, they are difficult or impossible to measure. Each individual's response is certain to change with age, environment, and even physiology.

Research has shown that in Western cultures adults, regardless of gender, prefer cooler tones of color: the most popular color preference is blue and the second is green. Small children, by contrast, prefer red followed by yellow or white. Around the age of eight, children begin to shift to the adult preferences for blue and green. In Japan, however, studies have shown that adults prefer the color red, followed by white, black, and yellow. In what context should we consider these preferences? Are we talking about fashion, interior design, color in nature, color in art? How does culture affect color preferences? Throughout history scientists and ethnologists have tried to pinpoint the essence of experiencing color. However, each small piece of information uncovered seems to lead to further questions.

A simple factor which has much to do with our confusion about color is the limits of language. Using words to describe a visual experience is inevitably difficult. If we are not trained in art and design, many of us have limited color vocabularies. We say we do not like yellow, and then walk into a room, notice the wall color, and exclaim, "This is beautiful . . . what color is this?" Of course, the answer is yellow. Yellow, it turns out, is a whole file of colors, and while many tones may seem unattractive, others look remarkably appealing. Too often color names are associated only with pure, intense hues; we need to develop a broader spectrum in our minds. Who has not spent time with mail-order catalogs trying to figure out which swatch of a T-shirt color is aubergine or cinnabar? The writers of catalog copy are to be credited with trying to build up our color vocabulary through word associations. However, it is clear that when we choose colors for our home, we are making decisions which will affect our comfort level for a longer period of time than our choice of a T-shirt, and the process can become a daunting task.

In considering color schemes for living spaces it is necessary to consider the purpose of the room, the geographical location, and the light sources. But perhaps most importantly, interior design decisions should hinge upon the preferences of those who will use the space. Comfort is key; individuality is important too. We all know what kind of environments make us feel content: those inner cues are excellent guides in making design decisions. Interior designers are most interested in how the color of a custom-made environment affects an individual's sense of well-being. The purpose of good design is ultimately to make people comfortable in their surroundings, whether at work or at leisure. ■

Design, previous pages (from left to right): Justine Ringlien, Sandra Nunnerley, Lila Levinson
Design, opposite: Justine Ringlien

Left: This close-up illustrates the precise detail that builds the aura of a space. Lampshades, accessories, and art objects are all like the strokes of an artist's paintbrush in coloring the comfort of a room. Design: Sandra Nunnerley

Opposite: Texture, light, and shadow add subtle variation to even the simplest neutral color schemes, which call attention to the intrinsic beauty of natural materials. The white-on-white dining area will relax and comfort its fortunate guests, training their eyes to more sensitive subject matter. Design: Pat Stotler

WHAT DESIGNERS SAY ABOUT THEIR EXPERIENCES WITH COLOR:

Professional interior designers are aware that color has a powerful effect on the mood of a room, and approach the problem of color selection in interesting ways. Lila Levinson of Accent on Design says, "I like to unite the interior and exterior spaces, and by using nature colors and texture I'm able to blur the boundaries between the two and visually enlarge the space by unifying it with the outdoors."

Left: This contemporary room has an unexpected color combination: the softest pink blush trimmed in gray. The gentle colors create a sense of quiet pleasure, the perfect setting for enjoying music from the nearby grand piano. Design: David A. Seglin

Opposite: A room is like a conversation; if it's about one thing it is boring—one color, one style, or one light intensity. Variety creates natural long-lasting interest. Design: Gail Shields-Miller

Carol Meltzer says, "Mood is very much about color, especially in Feng Shui design, which I do in addition to my regular projects. Certain colors create energy and can be used to stimulate, while other colors can create the feeling of tranquility. A work area may need the neutral tones and browns for 'grounding,' while a family room may need the vivid colors of a chintz floral in pink, green, [and] blue, colors which are friendly and create a relaxed atmosphere."

Left: A palette of many different tints and hues in the same space is sophisticated and requires more thoughtful planning, but is often worth the effort because the room will become a personal expression. Design: Sandra Nunnerley

Above: This is an interesting use of contrasting colors; they appear related because both the green hue and the orange hue contain strong yellow. The color intensity is the same, and the colors are actually close to each other (analogous) on the color wheel. Design: Ho Sang Shin

Designer Barbara Eberlein of Eberlein Design Consultants, Ltd. believes that "While a designer employs many methods to create the aura of a room, nothing establishes the mood faster and more unmistakably than color. Careful attention is paid not only to hue, but equally to value, reflectivity, and color interaction."

Above: This complex and comfortable room demonstrates how tinting colors softens their impact and allows more variety in a color palette. Pink is a tint of red, lilac a tint of purple, seafoam green a tint of green. With a few touches of deep color accents the result is harmonious and marvelously inviting. Design: Ronald Bricke

Opposite: A collector's look is achieved with a varied color scheme of contrasting colors that make each piece of furniture stand apart and establishes a varied natural palette in the large areas of the window treatments. Design: Diane Alpern Kovacs

"The myriad ways color is experienced includes our societal influences, cultural and historical events, the environmental movement, and so on, as well as our immediate surroundings and environment. I look to the architecture, to my clients' lifestyles and needs, and to the sophistication of the space to help determine how one would want to feel when entering an environment. Color plays a major role in creating that feeling," says Stacey Lapuk, of Stacey Lapuk Interior Design, Inc.

Left: A pleasant soft tone of blue-green reflects the sensitivity of a caring homeowner and the skill of a highly talented professional designer. This passageway of deftly tinted color and contrasting white architectural trim frames a delightful complementary palette within a welcome retreat. Design: Gail Shields-Miller

Opposite: The earthy tones of terra cotta, sisal fiber and stone are natural companions with green. The forest and the jungle are natural classrooms for colorists. Design: Lila Levinson

Designer Marshall Burstein suggests: *"Every individual has a specific goal for the use of their room. When creating a color scheme, clients are asked specific questions regarding the use of the room; [whether for] functions such as entertaining, relaxing, family gatherings, or their own personal getaway. Analyzing this perspective sets the 'tone' for selecting the right colors which reflect the personality or mood of the room."*

CHAPTER TWO

Color Theory for Interior Design

———◆———◆———

Professional interior designers use their understanding of basic color theory to compose the colors in a space much as artists use the same knowledge to compose the colors in a work of art. The relationships of the various pigment colors are easily understood if one studies a color wheel. The pages following present a fundamental vocabulary of the language of color, as well as practical, interactive theory for color usage.

The Language of Color

THE PRIMARY PIGMENT COLORS are red, blue, and yellow. All other colors derive from them. These three colors are universal in their appeal, appearing in some form in color palettes from nearly every historical period and from many diverse cultures. Comfort is often associated with the familiar, and the primary colors are familiar. Depending on geographic locale they may have different symbolic connotations, but they readily communicate with the human spirit.

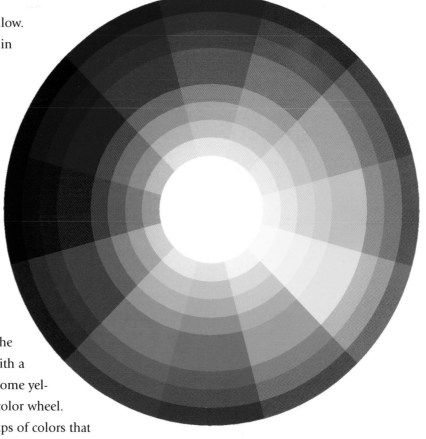

The second group of familiar colors are the secondary colors. These colors are formed by mixing equal parts of two primaries: blue and yellow make green, red and yellow make orange, and red and blue make violet. On the color wheel the secondary colors are located halfway between the primaries.

The third group of colors is called tertiary colors or intermediate colors; these are formed by mixing equal parts of a primary and a secondary color. In a standard twelve-segment color wheel, the intermediate colors are named by connecting their parent colors with a hyphen, using the primary color name first: yellow and orange become yellow-orange. There are six intermediate colors in a twelve-segment color wheel. From these basics interior designers develop color schemes or groups of colors that harmonize with each other.

Design, previous pages (from left to right): Patricia Bonis, Sandra Nunnerley, Sandra Nunnerley
Design, opposite: Patricia Bonis

Left: This distinctive and strong, highly personal room was created with the use of an unusual triad scheme. The depth, intensity, and contrast are exciting, but the careful balance of the bold color elements is reassuring.
Design: Ellen Lemer Korney

Opposite: This close-up view in a seating area shows how a skillful designer weaves a triad palette through the surfaces of various fabrics and accessories to create vibrancy and a subtle harmony within diverse elements.
Design: Patricia Bonis

In addition to considering the basic hues and their relationships in a color scheme, designers take into consideration the value (lightness and darkness), and the intensity (brightness and dullness) of colors. The value is changed by adding white to form tints or by adding black to form shades. The intensity of a color is altered by adding its complement (opposite on the color wheel) to lower its strength. Because all colors may be changed in these ways, it is possible to adapt any color to suit the purposes of the space where it will be used, to harmonize with other colors, to avoid monotony of tone, and to please the intended users of the space. ■

USING TRIADS TO FORM
COLOR RELATIONSHIPS:

Lines connecting the three primary and the three secondary colors on the color wheel form equal-sided triangles or triads. Triads are a way of achieving a balanced color scheme; they may be formed with any three colors which are equidistant on the color wheel, as well as with tints, shades, and different intensities of such colors.

Left: This is a stunning use of the three primaries to balance the color scheme in an elegant living space. A deeper tone of red on the walls harmonizes with medium-tone yellow draperies, and a paler blue in the striped sofas and carpet borders. The fireplace accent wall, the floors, and ceiling are white, keeping the space airy and inviting, while featuring the art and exquisite antiques. Design: Barbara Eberlein

Right: This inviting sitting room takes its color cue from the natural light pouring in through generous windows. The designer composed a color scheme based on primary hues, with blue and red tinted to a medium tone and arranged artfully on soft upholstered furniture, and the palest yellow tints the walls. Design: Sue Wenk

Opposite: A classic combination of violet and gold is skillfully balanced in this intimate space. The hues of ripe harvest fruits collected in a compote might have been the inspiration for this sophisticated color scheme. Design: Sandra Nunnerley

Right: A dramatic wallcovering in a large-scale print in tones of complementary red and olive is enhanced by exquisitely patterned fabrics in similar colors for draperies, upholstery, and carpet. The result is a brilliant and memorable dining room, where pleasurable conversations are certain to take place. Design: Gail Shields-Miller

Below: In this harmonious setting the architecture presents complementary tones of red and green in wood paneling and the mantle trim, and these colors are repeated in upholstery fabric and accessories. Design: Diane Alpern Kovacs

USING COMPLEMENTARY COLORS:

Another way to achieve a balanced color scheme is to use complementary colors. Any pair of colors directly opposite each other on the color wheel are complements and will naturally harmonize with each other. Mixtures of a color and its complement will produce less intense or grayed versions of the original color. When equal parts of a color and its complement are mixed, the resulting hue will look completely neutral and may be described as gray or putty.

Opposite: In this special bedroom the color scheme is developed from various tints of rose and its complement, a soft leaf green. The deeper rose on the floor and upholstered bench is balanced with medium tones on the walls and other upholstered pieces and white on the bedcover, woodwork, and ceiling. These colors are especially compatible because they are derived from the complements red and green. Design: Barbara Eberlein

Right: The ceiling is an area often overlooked as potential for drama, contrast, or special interest. The mottled burnt orange ceiling complements the pale, soft blue-green walls for a peaceful glow. Each surface achieves depth through pattern or texture. Design: Stanford R. Thigpen

Below: The deep warm wood tones in this paneled sitting area are enhanced and complemented by the designer's choice of cool green upholstery fabrics and a light neutral floor covering, an excellent example of the effective use of a complementary color scheme. Design: Patricia Bonis

Left: A fundamentally monochromatic scheme can be very refined and interesting. Tints, textures, and patterns add the variety needed to achieve a satisfying environment. Gold is a fail-proof trim when using rich neutral colors. Design: Sandra Nunnerley

Opposite: A masterful arrangement of textures and patterns makes this sunny sleeping room warm and inviting—a space guaranteed to lift the spirits. Design: Anthony Antine

Below: Soothing and soft, the simple lines and cool colors offer a respite from the blazing natural light on the exterior balcony. The designer avoids high contrast, using a monochromatic color scheme with pale tones of lilac modulating to silvery white for a refreshing and original effect. Design: Barbara Eberlein

USING MONOCHROMATIC COLORS:

The third way to create a pleasing color scheme is to use only one color, but to introduce variations of that color, altering either its lightness or darkness (value) by adding white or black, or by adding its complement. Such schemes are called monochromatic, as they are based on one color.

Left: This bright analogous color scheme is designed to reverse from blue and green for visiting boys to peach and yellow for visiting girls. Young children love active vivid colors, so this is an appropriate, as well as clever, color solution. Design: Allison Holland

Opposite: A unique space with an appropriate artistic analogous color scheme featuring soft tones of blue, blue-green, green, and gold with the palest yellow-textured walls. Delicate and friendly, these unusual colors create a romantic setting. Design: Sandra Nunnerly

Below: The appeal of analogous or "friendly" colors is clear in this cozy and inviting sitting area where a warm palette of reds, oranges, and yellows creates the perfect atmosphere for staying at home by the fire. Design: William Eubanks

USING ANALOGOUS COLORS:

———————◆◆◆———————

A fourth way to achieve a color scheme that has visual harmony is to use three to five colors which are adjacent to each other on the color wheel. These analogous color schemes are sometimes referred to as "hot" or "cool," because by choosing neighboring colors, the result will convey one effect or the other.

Opposite: A subtle modulation of warm colors moving from red to red-violet to grape in a variety of textures, and punctuated with a blue accent on the lampshade creates a soft, comfortable retreat in this original setting. Design: Gary Gibson

Right: A complex interplay of analogous warm colors and textures from flax to deep red plush create an inviting seating area. The buttery walls contribute to the glowing comfort. Design: Sandra Nunnerley

Below: Comfortable analogous colors include the rich brown tones of the elegant wood trim in this stately Tudor room. Floral and stripe fabrics and lovely natural light enliven the space. Design: Diane Alpern Kovacs

Left: A single color, perhaps inspired by the handsome painting shown beside the fireplace, is repeated in a variety of textures in fabrics, as well as on the walls, the painted furniture, and even the mats on the smaller framed works of art. A peaceful, unified effect results, making the room a haven, serene and secure. Design: Barbara Eberlein

Opposite: A monochromatic color scheme (in this case based on neutral wood tones) can be enlivened with small doses of a brilliant color accent through art, flowers, or accessories. Design: Patricia Bonis

Below: In this complex yet appealing color scheme the designer uses yellow-checked wallpaper as a neutral background, setting the tone for merrymaking. Against the "neutral" he pairs a less familiar complementary pair, red-orange and blue-green, as well as tints of the complements red and green, in an unlikely but masterful combination which resembles a summer garden in full flower. Design: Ho Sang Shin

FURTHER HINTS ON CREATING COMFORTABLE COLOR SCHEMES:

The colors as they appear on the color wheel are pure, and in large areas may be too intense to create a comfortable space for living. So interior designers often compensate for too much intensity by tinting or graying at least one of the colors in a color scheme. They also consider the size of the area where a color will be used. Very intense color is often reserved for relatively small areas, to provide an accent in larger areas of less intense color.

A point to remember in developing a color scheme is to include the colors of natural architectural features in all plans. Woodwork, ceilings, fireplace construction, and floors all count as colors and must be considered when balancing a color scheme.

CHAPTER THREE

Creating Comfort with Neutrals

———◆◆◆———

Neutral tones were formed with the earliest pigments used by man, who borrowed from nature the natural powders and fluids of earth and plants, fruits, and even animal blood and shellfish. Perhaps this is why basic neutral colors, black, white, brown, and gray, have accumulated many symbolic meanings in human cultures. Many neutral tones seem to derive from the colors of the surfaces of the earth itself, and this may also contribute to the feelings of comfort they inspire. These colors appear familiar and friendly in interior spaces; we are creatures of the earth. ■

Opposite: A "guest color" two-toned striped blue fabric lifts an otherwise neutral palette of beige and brown. Neutral backgrounds are perfect foils for accent colors. Design: Anthony Antine

Right: A cutting-edge modern dining space is sculptural in its simplicity, with no frivolous details. An aquamarine hue emanates from the large painting to the glass table top. This sophisticated setting provides an unobtrusive background for colorful conversations with family and guests. Design: Barbara Eberlein

Below: Sleek contemporary simplicity echoes the international "less is more" philosophy in a nearly monochromatic color palette of beige and taupe. Design: Barbara Eberlein

NATURAL NEUTRALS:

Designer John Sutton says "The colors we see most in nature are 'safe'—blue of the sky and ocean, green of the trees. Particularly in areas of the country where we strive to bring the outdoors in, using colors seen outside will extend the interior, out."

Design, previous pages (from left to right): Anthony Antine, Jill Vantosh, Stacey Lapuk
Design, opposite: Anthony Antine

Right: Simplicity and order are reassuring to the human spirit. Here natural light, natural wood and clay tones, and a golden white glowing on the painted wall create a friendly and inviting space. Design: Gayle Reynolds

Opposite: A hand-painted trompe l'oeil floor featuring a carpet with assorted flowers and berries defines this sunny yellow breakfast area that is anchored by a deeper green hutch. Design: Anne Tarasoff

Below: The tropical greens and clay-tiled roof colors come right inside over the balcony into this palette of earthy naturals. Design: Lila Levinson

WHAT DESIGNERS SAY ABOUT THEIR EXPERIENCES WITH NEUTRALS:

Many designers mention colors from nature as a source for neutral palettes. Al Dickerson says: "Most people are comfortable in natural settings. Light blues, light roses, suede whites and browns work best, with various green accents. I find that green is a balancing color evoking feelings of comfort and relaxation. I never recommend stark white or blue for clients in this situation, these colors are too cold; similarly reds are too hot."

Noticing Neutrals

NEUTRAL COLORS ARE ALWAYS under the influence of the light and colors nearby, and so they may go unnoticed, acting as backdrops for more dramatic and intense hues, for strong contrasts of light and dark tones, or for subtle changes in texture. They are, however, of paramount importance in developing comfortable color schemes.

Often the color tones of natural woodwork, floors, and masonry cannot be altered, and must be incorporated into the color plan for a space. Before beginning to choose new colors, a meticulous inventory of these elements needs to be taken, and the light sources for the space must be considered as well. In nearly every case the largest areas of color will act as neutrals, so careful selection of these tones is the first step toward building a successful combination of colors.

Most designers prefer natural tones for floor coverings because of the large areas involved and the expense and durability of the products used. Neutrals allow for flexibility in both furnishings and use of space, and are generally less troublesome to maintain.

For the same reasons many individuals decide to use neutral colors on their walls as well. While using "safe" neutrals may be a starting point, there are many things to consider in developing a color scheme. ▪

A beige color palette creates a receding background for the "punch" of bright colors in the art and accessory pillows. Design: Pedro Rodriguez; Opposite: Jill Vantosh

Opposite: A grand Western view is the benchmark for the palette of desert earth tones in this airy living room. Design: Stephanie Walters

Right: Most clients prefer neutral color palettes to serve the needs of cleanliness and functionality. Everyone appreciates beautifully finished cabinetry. Design: Lila Levinson

Below: An amazing Tudor-style window with leaded glass sets a high level of expectation for the contents of this room. The palette is restrained and draws one's eye toward the extraordinary architectural detailing. Design: Carole Weaks

CHECKLIST FOR CREATING COLOR COMFORT

Before selecting colors for a color scheme, think about:

- the purpose of the space
- the size of the space
- the light sources in the space
- architectural elements whose colors cannot easily be altered
- the furnishings and accessories that are already owned and may be used in the space
- the people who will use the space, their personalities and preferences
- the time of day the space will most frequently be used
- the climate of the region and the changes in light it will produce
- the prevalent colors in window views.

Classic Neutrals

CLASSIC NEUTRALS ARE TIMELESS COLORS whose familiarity is comforting; they always reflect good taste and style.

Brown is a rich sensual color, suggesting earth and fertility. It also connotes roots and familial connections, the security of hearth and home. Brown tends to be quiet and passive, a receptor for more vivid accent colors or an attractive companion to other natural hues. There is a wide range of brown tones, from warm to cool, and from pale to dark. Beige is a popular pale variation of brown.

Black represents opposition to white or life, and is often associated with lifelessness or death. Although it represents a completely passive or inactive state and absorbs all colors rather than reflects them as white does, black has been an important and popular fashion color since the sixteenth century, connoting worldly strength and style. Because pure black stands out among other colors, it was recognized as effective in establishing individuality without appearing ribald. Perhaps it remains popular because of its power as a strong and sophisticated neutral, setting off and complementing nearby light and bright color areas. Black is not absolute; there are warm and cool, glossy and matte, deep and flat blacks. Its strength changes with its surroundings.

Gray is a noncommittal color, neither passive nor

Restful comfort and security are created by an elegantly draped canopy in white and tan. The room is also tan, with accents of black. Design: Gayle Reynolds; Opposite: Stacey Lapuk

sive, warm or cool, tense or relaxed. It stands between other colors, offering richness and sophistication. Grays are greatly affected by changes in light, and can be nudged toward cool or warm with small additions of red and yellow or blue and green. Gray is a stylish partner for more brilliant colors, cushioning their impact without detracting from their personalities.

White reflects all colors and is, therefore, the ultimate neutral. In some cultures it symbolizes life and hope; it also represents purity and goodness. White "goes with" any other color, but like the other neutrals there are many versions from which to choose; these include bright and dull, warm and cool, glossy and flat tones. In the Eskimo language there are over one hundred words for describing the fine gradations of white indigenous to the arctic landscape. ■

Opposite: This small den and media room features a chocolate wall covering. According to the designer, "At night this room is magical, and it has a very quiet, calm, 'cocoon-like' atmosphere." Design: Donna Dunn

Right: Informality and drama are both present in this bedroom, which integrates nature into the setting through a skylight and an arched window. A pine-paneled ceiling and a large pine cabinet contribute warmth without darkening the space. A patterned rug in muted tones and subtle bed dressings complete this loft bedroom. Design: Ellen Lemer Korney

Below: A small-scale library area, wrapped in natural wood tones, is cozy and inviting. The warm color expands the space, and the book covers add bright color accents. Design: Gayle Reynolds

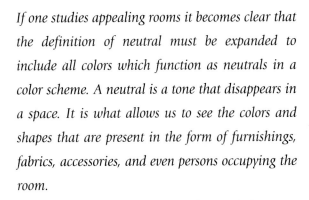

DESIGNERS EXPAND THE DEFINITION OF NEUTRALS:

If one studies appealing rooms it becomes clear that the definition of neutral must be expanded to include all colors which function as neutrals in a color scheme. A neutral is a tone that disappears in a space. It is what allows us to see the colors and shapes that are present in the form of furnishings, fabrics, accessories, and even persons occupying the room.

Designers use neutrals skillfully to help us see the drama and personality present in a space. They are courageous in using many colors as neutrals which do not fall into the classic definitions described above.

Left: Large areas of wood in a room are an important element in the color palette. These warm-hued paneled walls are a backdrop for brighter tones in the upholstery. Details such as pillows and accessories are effective ways to complete a color palette and add drama. Design: Patricia Bonis

Opposite: Natural neutrals abound in this Western-theme sleeping area through granite-colored floors, a variety of wood tones, and a luxuriant green private view. Design: Stephanie Walters

Below: A wall covering in a pale buttery yellow with a subtle pattern surrounds the rich wood tones. The textures of richly woven fabrics and floor coverings along with carefully chosen accessories in tobacco and black complete the range of values in a warm and informal atmosphere. Design: Barbara Eberlein

Marshall Burstein suggests, "A client who is unsure of their preference would be guided to use a neutral color scheme with accents within the green [section of the] color wheel. Shades of green are the most nonthreatening color of the entire spectrum."

Left: Walls, upholstery, and marble are unified by a single color, with the walls featuring a slightly lighter blush of the warm fabric tone. Design: Ronald Bricke

Opposite: Luxurious deep comfort is created against a mild backdrop of neutrals through the knowing use of exquisite detail in fabric, upholstery, accessories, and especially lighting. This bedroom defines comfortable color. Design: Jean Valente

Below: While it appears that there is almost no color in this room, the designer has used textures, accessories, and light to create depth and variety. Design: Justine Ringlien

According to Marcello Luzi of Weixler, Peterson and Luzi, "With a neutral background, clients can then 'dabble' in color, through accessories and collections until they become more sure and more confident about what they like."

Left: A close-up of a delicately modulated neutral color palette against a cream background that includes rust, leaf, and berry accents. The message is quiet comfort. Design: Phyllis Goldberg

Opposite: The palest pink tone pattern of circles in squares casts a glow in this most inviting seating area. Fabrics are off-white neutrals with pattern and textural accents on pillows and rug. Touches of gold add to the sumptuous effect. Here is a neutral room that is comfortable, but defintely not bland. Design: Brett Beldock

Below: The technique of layering subtle gradations of hue from cream to cinnamon makes an interesting palette, warm and comfortable. Design: Patricia Bonis

Designer Justine Ringlien sums up the idea of neutrals, observing, "Usually any color can be made workable if used in a 'grayed' form. In paint this would be achieved by adding its complement."

Opposite: Intricate detail of trompe l'oeil wall panels and a woven carpet all in the same celadon green against an especially appealing warm yellow guarantee a feeling of warmth and inspiration in this lovely setting. Design: Brett Beldock

Right: The neutral surroundings provide a backdrop for the focal point of the room, a beautiful fireplace. Design: Barbara Eberlein

Marshall Burstein points out that all shades of green are "frequently used in clothing because it looks good against all skin types and makes people feel good in their environment. Soft teals create a subtle effect, while hunter greens are more dramatic."

Left: Classical accents in architecture and accessories combine harmoniously in a cool, serene palette to create an atmosphere of power and restraint. Design: Vince Lattuca

Opposite: A bath tiled with dark and exotic stone colors and featuring brass fixtures emits a feeling of privacy and luxury—a personal retreat. Neutrals are comfortable in small spaces and complement skin tones effectively. Design: Gayle Reynolds

Below: The use of large areas of black creates drama, especially when combined with the contrast of pure white. Unusual in a bedroom, the effect is luxurious because of exquisite details in the moldings and the canopy. The black is echoed in the stone fireplace façade. Design: Ronald Bricke

Left: The largest areas in this room—walls, ceilings, draperies, upholstery, and bed dressings—are all almost the same tone of rich cream. But far from being boring, the billowing draperies and graceful flowing canopy lift the mood of this comfortable space. Design: Susan Lovelace

Below: Against a pattern created by two tints of delicate pink, a weighty sculptural table flanked by chairs in contrasting light and dark colors offers a range of tones in a restrained palette. Objets d'art show beautifully in this exquisite setting. Design: Brett Beldock

Opposite: A spectacular panoramic view of New York City from this pied-à-terre is all that is needed for accent and drama with a black and white palette. Design: Ronald Bricke

Opposite: In this indoor/outdoor room the walls, furniture, and fabrics are kept in unobtrusive neutral tones which will blend with the changing color scheme of the surrounding natural setting. Design: Barbara Eberlein

Right: This dining room summarizes the "California look" with a neutral color palette, the contemporary treatment of traditional styles, upholstered comfort, and dramatic highlights. Design: Donna Dunn

Below: A harmony of neutral tones creates a soothing bedroom which is both refreshing and elegant, with a brown and white traditional floral pattern, a tone-on-tone beige stripe, and black accents against crisp white walls. Design: Patricia Bonis

Designer Cheryl Van Duyne often chooses "neutral colors as such soft, warm grays and earth colors. Most people are comfortable with these colors and find them peaceful and long-lasting."

Left: A billowy soft bed with lavish pillows in colors ranging from white to sand, taupe, cinnamon, and black suggest ultimate comfort, a personal retreat. Design: Stacey Lapuk

Below: Intricately sewn pillows with rich detail, pecan-colored walls, tasseled window treatments, and textured fabrics combine in a lively arrangement featuring interest and dimension. The room is inviting and harmonious, a place to feel at ease. Design: Diane Alpern Kovacs

Interior designers define a neutral as any color which is used as a background for other colors and textures. Anthony Antine, of Antine Associates, Inc., recommends yellow. "It seems to go with everything and most people like it," he says.

Right: A rich, sand-colored monochromatic palette unifies walls, fabrics, wood finishes, and accessories, with pinpoint accent colors and taupe trims to relieve the monotony. Design: Justine Ringlien

Below: This monochromatic buff room is an elegant place for entertaining. Comfort is established in the deep plush carpet and the richly cushioned upholstery. The piano suggests the pleasure of listening to beautiful sounds in a beautiful setting. Design: Donna Dunn

Opposite left: Neutral palettes need not be boring. This elegant bedroom has a varied palette in a narrow range of subtle tints of taupe and cinnamon, along with gold and black accents. The pièce de résistance sleigh bed is upholstered and covered in a small-scale plaid in cinnamon and black. There is a five-paneled antique Oriental screen at the head of the bed, and an Empire three-legged black table rests beside a taupe upholstered daybed. The color scheme is consistent, and the details are carefully planned, making this room a triumph. Design: Stacey Lapuk

Below: White everywhere except the floors is relieved by plum and black plaid upholstery on a French chair and vivid turquoise floral print pillows on the sofa. Design: Steven M. Hefner

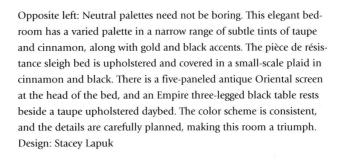

Opposite: Large Oriental carpets tie together rooms with butter-colored walls, camel-colored upholstery, and accents of Chinese red repeating the color of the floor covering. Design: Nancy Craig Hollingsworth

Right: Soft damask tone-on-tone upholstery creates an atmosphere of comfort in a simple room where neutrals act as a backdrop for art objects. Design: Sandra Nunnerley

"A neutral palette always provides a good color foundation for the client who is unsure of color," says Marcello Luzi of Weixler, Peterson and Luzi. *"However, many light or pastel tones can serve the same purpose and can provide a 'hint' of color without overpowering the space. But it must be color that's not too saturated."*

CHAPTER FOUR

Creating Comfort with Primary Colors

———◆◆◆———

E veryone's familiarity with the primary colors, in addition to their association with beauty in nature, make red, blue, and yellow enduringly popular for interior design in nearly every culture. Used singly or in combination, the range of tones for each of the basic three allows for versatility in achieving a comfortable effect. Often the colors are tinted or their intensity is tamed or muted for larger areas, and the pure tones are reserved for accent.

Red Rooms

RED IS AN OLD COLOR. Historically, it was one of the first to attract the human eye, as evidenced in prehistoric art and artifacts from ancient civilizations. In the West, red is second only to blue in popularity, and in Japan it is the most popular color. The Egyptians used red ochre, an earthy tone created from earth pigments, to color their bodies, walls, and certain fabrics. Later, red dyes were extracted and manufactured from insects and such plants as cinnabar. Madder root became a particularly important source of red pigment in Europe during the sixteenth century. In the twentieth century synthetic red sources such as alizarin and cadmium were discovered, adding to the range of tones available to produce paints and dyes.

Psychologically, red conveys the most potent image of all the colors, the pulse of life itself, surging with intensity, raising the heart rate and the blood pressure. Active and aggressive, passionate red presses us toward success and achievement. It represents the enormity of desire in the present moment, and is associated with warmth and fire.

Symbolically, red is an assertive color that attracts attention and suggests power. As the color of blood, it is associated with the heart and love, but it also may be an expression of rage or murder. It has often been a favored color for mili-

Frontier red looks cheerful and friendly in an informal Western-style guest bedroom. The authenticity of bright red harmonizes with the natural wood tones. Design: Allison Holland

Design, previous pages (from left to right): Brett Beldock, Al Evans, J. Staff
Design, opposite: Brett Beldock

tary uniforms, perhaps to hide the wounds of battle, but certainly to strike fear in the enemy through its suggestion of confidence. It is universally the color to alert and halt us—with the exception of China, where red means go.

Red is the most emotional of the primary colors, but its effects are varied. Depending on the tone, this color can be exciting or warm or elegant. Interior designers choose more intense tones of red for active rooms where lively conversations and interactions are expected. Subdued, warm colors relax occupants and invite openness and friendliness, making red a favorite color for dining rooms. If the intended use of the room is more tranquil, red can be tinted to a more discreet value of rose or pink for softness and subtlety.

Soft pink expands the space in a room and provides billowy feminine comfort, while deep maroons and burgundies produce a rich masculine effect. When red is combined with orange, lively optimistic spaces are created, and when it is combined with blue, mysterious and dreamy effects result. Red combined with its complement green is classically elegant; our eyes revel in the fittingness of this association. The use of bright red with bright blue and white is also a timeless combination which symbolizes loyalty and is always stylish.

Although fashion dictates a particular tone of red each year as being au courant, the basic hue is forever a source of satisfaction and delight, because of its warm and positive properties. ■

Opposite: Gradations of velvety pink convey softness and quiet in an enchanted sleeping room fit for a princess. Design: Al Evans

Right: Rich cranberry walls delineate a young man's retreat. The bedcovering in a contrasting tint of indigo, with a plaid accent fabric on the pillows and windows, and with a boldly striped rug, all achieve a youthful and informal style. Design: Lise Lawson

Below: A cozy country seating area is warmed by rose red walls and an informal printed fabric with cream background. This room proves the diverse effects possible with red, from very formal to relaxed informal. Design: Allison Holland

Designer Gayle Reynolds says, "I once used a rich, rose red striated on the walls of a young, fast-paced professional couple's living room. The couple loved being in the room. They felt it was both a relaxing space and a great social room. The pink tone of the stripe had a calming effect, while the red tone was stimulating and exciting."

Left: For the imaginative, a spectacular color in an unusual space makes an individual, personal, and unique statement. Design: Susie Leader

Opposite: Pink, a tint of red, becomes a subtle background for other pastel colors. The effect of red is varied by its intensity and its tint. Design: Sue Wenk

Designer Lynn Robinson says, "I especially love cherry red or a rich color in living and dining rooms. Vibrant colors are very apt to create an atmosphere of intimacy and warmth, stimulating conversation....My own living room has cherry red walls with pure white trim on doors, windows, and moldings. Several people have commented on how lively charity meetings as well as parties are in that room. Although the look is elegant, the colors tend to stimulate people in a nice way."

Left: A rich red sofa is the pièce de résistance in this stylish and dramatic living room, defined by gold and silver textured walls and elegant black lacquer furnishings. Design: Pedro Rodriguez

Opposite: Red walls and gilt trim along with a sparkling crystal chandelier combine to suggest the highest level of elegance and formality. The fabulous gold and yellow upholstered chairs complete a setting fit for royalty. Design: Anthony Antine

Below: This intimate space is warmed with pink-toned walls and terra-cotta-tiled floors, a creative background for an eclectic collection of furnishings. Design: Justine Ringlien

Anne Tarasoff of Anne Tarasoff Interiors says "Red was the color selected by a client stating that it made her happiest when she wore red or stayed in a red room."

Barbara Eberlein of Eberlein Design Consultants, Ltd. describes "jewel-like, saturated burgundy walls [as] evocative of the nineteenth century and its preference for strong color and complex mixture of pattern."

Opposite: Restful red on rose-blush walls is a backdrop for the deep red of a mahogany armoire, the glowing red of a Chinese needlepoint carpet, the straw-colored and pale pink floral chintz and striped fabrics, as well as a pristine white antique lace bed-cover. These subtle modulations are the structure of a complex monochromatic color scheme. Design: Ellen Lemer Korney

Right: A deep shade of red on these library walls evokes a mood of tranquility and warmth for a comfortable retreat. Design: Ronald Bricke

Designer Laura Bohn cautions, "Red and strong hues in general draw too much attention to the walls of the room. I use strong colors as accents only, but never all over. They take up too much space and make the room too vibrant."

Left: The cherry walls and chair upholstery fabric shown here are beautiful by day or by night in this traditional dining room. Red is often chosen for dining areas because of its hospitable warmth. It seems to invite lively conversation. Design: Sue Wenk

Opposite: Lipstick-red walls with white ceilings and woodwork are balanced by dark finished wood. The room strikes a festive atmosphere for entertaining. Design: Lynn Robinson

"Deep rich colors such as burgundy, red, and hunter green add drama and warmth to an elegant room," says Anthony Antine of Antine Associates, Inc.

"Reds create a lot of heat and hyper energy. This can be hard to live with, especially for high-pressured, elderly, or ill people," comments designer Carol Meltzer.

Blue Rooms

BLUE HAS BEEN WIDELY USED in interior design since the time of the Egyptians. In Western culture Greeks and Romans included blues in their palettes, and blues were a prominent element in the brilliant jewel-like color schemes of the Renaissance. The French kings drew from the Renaissance. They included blue within the palette of their favorite colors—particularly the pastel tones favored by Madame Pompadour. As for the English, their preferred shade of blue leaned toward green in the earlier Georgian period, while the majestic and classic Wedgwood blue reigned in the late Georgian period. American style and color preferences were naturally influenced by the French and English in colonial times, so blue has always been considered a standard color. More recently paint manufacturing technology has allowed the production of literally hundreds of tints of the basic colors, so the choice of blues ranges from the palest, coolest tints to the very deep, most intense tones.

Blue is a color of contrasts. Although tones of blue are perceived in vast areas of nature in sky and water, natural blue pigments are relatively rare, and therefore, expensive.

Blue is capable of creating the striking quality of great depth, an aspect which was valued by Renaissance masters like Leonardo da Vinci. Yet in addition to its capacity for

A dining room that is used for entertaining can afford to be impressive and slightly formal, an effect achieved with these rich Prussian blue walls. The dining table adds another layer of colorful interest and focus to this space. Design: Barbara Eberlein; opposite: Al Evans

expressing airiness, it can also suggest the cold solidity of slate. Blue is described as a cool color, but high-intensity blues are used to suggest electric energy.

The psychological effect of blue is serenity, a deep peace, and contentment. The mood evoked is introspective, calling us inward to a more spiritual place. In some cultures a deep tone of blue is recommended for meditation. Contentment means feeling stress free and unified. A sense of belonging induces the response of loyalty, a word often associated with blue, as in "true blue." Deep blue also suggests the qualities of security and strength, and as such, it is often chosen as a uniform color for police and the military. By contrast, lighter tints of blue evoke femininity, tranquility, and tenderness.

Contemplation of blue seems to have a healing effect on the body, lowering blood pressure, respiration, and heart rates, but this color also sensitizes people, making them more vulnerable to strong emotions and pain, hence the popular phrase, "feeling blue."

Opposite: Here is a pensive retreat for intimate communications and journal writing amid soft low-intensity blue, faded elegance with antique white. Design: Lila Levinson

Right: A warm midnight blue, the color of a clear night sky, bordered with a lighter shade on the wall trim wraps this blue-on-blue room. This palette welcomes family and guests with reassurance in a balance between casual and formal mood. A room for all reasons. Design: Ronald Bricke

Pale blue recedes in a space, opening up the walls and extending the perception of a room's area. By contrast, dark blue closes in the walls and creates a feeling of solace and security. Mixing blue with its neighbor green produces fresh and pleasant harmonies; mixing blue with its neighbor violet produces mystery and excitement. The intensity of blue is altered by adding orange or one of its sister colors, red-orange or yellow-orange.

Blue is recommended by many designers for sleeping rooms because of its naturally restful and solitary qualities.

In these spaces the tone may be light or dark, as long as the intensity of the color is not too high. In more active living spaces, blue is best when combined with other colors to avoid the cold and bland effect of a monochromatic blue color scheme. Blue with yellow evokes a friendly and lively atmosphere, blue with green suggests freshness and nature, blue with red suggests tradition and gaiety, blue with orange suggests richness and conviviality, and blue with violet suggests the exotic and the mysterious. ■

Left: This is a very sophisticated hue, with less of the traditional blue, romantic mood, but nevertheless very comforting. The pink bed cover is a skillful contrast. Design: Ronald Bricke

Right: A palette of medium blue and white is certain to be crisp, highlighting the interesting architecture of the ceiling and bringing a contemporary simplicity to this eclectic room. Design: Ronald Bricke

WHAT DESIGNERS SAY ABOUT
THEIR EXPERIENCES WITH BLUE:

Designer Cheryl Van Duyne described redesigning a master bedroom in which "the walls had been soft pink. The color I selected for the walls was soft blue/green. My clients were amazed at how open and peaceful the room seemed and how much 'larger' it was."

Left: Vivid blue is freshened with crisp white accents for a clean and dramatic effect in this room. Design: Steven M. Hefner

Opposite: A dark, rich blue dominates this palette, but patterns of red with painted white woodwork build a casual mood. The varied hues bring interest to the space and avoid monotony. Design: Sue Wenk

Below: This traditional all-over toile print of fine fabric and wallcovering achieves both drama and the security of a monochromatic palette. This is a formula that rarely fails to please, especially in a bedroom. An authentic documented print is an extra assurance of quality. Design: Jean Valente

Designer Nancy Craig Hollingsworth reports that "one recuperating client who had little interest in decorating found a blue and white room particularly peaceful."

Opposite: An artfully hand-painted light blue wall with elegant floral swags is a dream-like background for the crisp red and green floral print fabric in a bedroom worthy of many regenerative hours. Design: Anne Tarasoff

Left, Below: A romantic mood is achieved through the delicate use of floral trompe l'oeil in misty blue with more intense tints of blue in the fabric and carpet. Design: Anne Tarasoff

From designer Al Dickerson: "One client really loved the color blue. Because she was warm, outgoing, and friendly, I was concerned the cool color would potentially 'turn off' conversation when used in her entertainment spaces. I suggested adding another warmer color to better reflect her personality. We added peach (a gregarious and outgoing tone), which created the warm, personal, and relaxed space she had hoped for."

Yellow Rooms

YELLOW GLOWS, SHINES, AND SPARKLES;
its effect is unmistakably cheerful. It reflects light and also
emits light. Yellow is not only a guaranteed spirit lifter, but
yellow light also allows the most efficient viewing with the
human eye.

The research of Dr. Max Lüscher, author of *The Lüscher
Color Test*, has shown that a preference for yellow expresses
an expansiveness, a letting down or relaxation of tension. It
suggests release from problems, harassment, and restrictions.
Yellow also conveys the hope or expectation of greater happi-
ness and positive change. It is a color which looks ahead
toward the future—a bright future, an optimistic future.

The history of symbolic messages communicated by
yellow is varied. The lightest and brightest color in the spectrum, it suggests energy and the sun as well as gold and
wealth. Metallic gold, a form of yellow, suggested spirituality
in Byzantine art, and was a popular background color during
the Renaissance.

People of desert regions have a wide range of words
to describe tones of yellow indigenous to their environment,
indicating their sensitivity to this color's subtleties. Yet
Roman writers scarcely mentioned its existence.

In China's Ch'ing dynasty (A.D. 1644–1912) yellow
was reserved for the emperor, but because yellow crosses

This tint of lemon yellow is a perfect
background for traditional interiors
of predominantly English eighteenth-
century heritage. The gloss-white trim
provides a crisp border for the painted
walls, calling attention to the well-
mannered architectural detail of this
room. Design: Anthony Antine;
opposite, John Staff

identified plague victims in the Middle Ages, yellow became synonymous with contagious disease. Clearly, the symbolic messages of color are often contradictory; one must always consider the context of time and place.

Although yellow lags behind blue, green, and red in popularity in most Western cultures, it ranks just behind red, black, and white, as one of the most favored colors in Japan.

Interior designers use many versatile variations of yellow to create expressive effects. Used full strength it can be unsettling in a large area, but its power is easily subdued by reducing the size of intense color areas, by tinting (the addition of

white), or by changing the intensity through the addition of its complement, violet.

Yellow can be nudged toward a warmer or cooler effect by adding one of the other two primaries. Yellow tones range from yellow greens—similar to the color of celery and artichoke hearts when blue is added—to yellow-oranges resembling pumpkins and apricots when red is added.

A lively neutral when lightened or dulled, yellow evokes nature and harmony when combined with greens, the freshness of sea and sky when combined with blues, and reassuring earthiness when combined with oranges and browns. ■

Opposite: An eclectic interior combines stylistic elements from many sources, here carried into the unusual color palette of yellow and blue. Proving the versatility of yellow, this entranceway of a very elegant home unifies the many fine details of architecture and furnishings. Although the setting is formal, the mood is friendly and approachable. Design: Stanford R. Thigpen

Right: Bright, light lemon yellow in this breakfast room is optimistic in its effect, using clean, crisp, defined color for sunny daytime use. Design: Barbara Eberlein

Below: Yellow fixtures accent the sophistication of classic black and white in this stylish contemporary bath. The liveliness of yellow energizes the space. Design: John Berenson

WHAT DESIGNERS SAY ABOUT THEIR EXPERIENCES WITH YELLOW:

Susie Leader of Susie Leader Interiors says, "The clients tell us that the soft butterscotch color which we used on all the walls and ceiling in their huge great room created a warm and intimate atmosphere, in spite of the room's huge size."

Left: A very delicate tint of yellow is both background and foreground in this contemporary home, adding simplicity with a classic mood of elegance. At this low level of intensity the color has a buttery, neutral presence which is especially comforting and inviting. Design: Ronald Bricke

Opposite: The warmth of yellow invites conversation in a chic, contemporary living space. The upholstered chairs and the color suggest comfort without sacrificing style. Design: John Berenson

Says designer Lila Levinson of Accent on Design, "There was a small, north bedroom painted a cool white which seemed dark and depressing. We painted the walls yellow and trim bright white. The room then had a warm, cheery and sunny feeling and became the favorite bedroom!"

Left: Guests will certainly be inspired by the overscale crystal chandelier and the round mahogany dining table bathed in the classic yellow glow of this extraordinary room. The mood is inviting and stimulating, one which will lift everyone's expectations for animated conversation. Design: Anthony Antine

Opposite: A subtle checkered pattern of two yellow tints in the wallcovering sets the informal mood in this game room. The walls are a suitable background for a wide range of cheerful complementary and analogous colors, part of a very eclectic theme. Design: Ho Sang Shin

Below: Cheerful yellow is an excellent choice for a small room, such as this guest bath, where it expands the walls and infuses light into the warm wood tones. Colors in the fabric and wallpaper are balanced for variety. An abrupt juxtaposition would be uncomfortable in this small and personal a space. Design: Allison Holland

Designer Carol Meltzer says, "Many people think kitchens should be 'happy' rooms and that means yellow to them. Yellow can create a good deal of heat energy, and in a kitchen which tends to be used a good deal and which gets intense sunshine, this might be the wrong choice."

YELLOW ROOMS · 107

Opposite: An appetizing combination of cozy furnishings and an almost yellow-green wall color suggests the wholesome events and family meals that will enliven this joyful space. The flowers have been selected to echo the "guest colors" in the room. This environment suggests a host who cares about every aspect of how family and friends are served. Design: Allison Holland

Right: A medium-intensity choice of yellow paint, slightly lighter than the rich yellow stripe in the simply elegant drapery fabric, lights the walls to an unobtrusive glow. Several subtle neutrals from a different region of the color spectrum prove the versatility of this color choice as either a background or an accent. Design: Patricia Bonis

Below: This is a quite proper English living room, where yellow is a backdrop for fine eighteenth-century furnishings and for an array of carefully chosen accessories. This limited palette contributes to a sense of order, which is a required ingredient in many well-planned homes. Design: Barbara Eberlein

Left: Yellow lightens and brightens this space and adds subtle detail through faint trompe l'oeil on the paneled walls. Fabric colors are varied from deep green velvet to warmer tones of yellow and analogous salmon hues. Gold is an effective and luxurious accent in this rich palette. Design: Anthony Antine

Opposite: Details always make the difference. Colorful accents of green, black, and tortoise add dimension to the all-over yellow scheme. Design: Anthony Antine

Below: The yellow palette is extended with more neutrals through a personal collection of accessories. This space will provide a mood lift throughout every season of the year. Design: Patricia Bonis

CHAPTER FIVE

Creating Comfort with Secondary Colors

T he secondary colors, green, orange, and violet, while not quite as commonly used as the primaries, nevertheless are frequently chosen for interior design projects because of their familiarity and pleasant associations. Green is the most popular of the three. For more conservative colorists paler, less-intense tones are recommended for large areas. All three of the pure hues are effective accent colors for neutral palettes.

Green Rooms

THE COLOR GREEN IS REFRESHING, soothing, cool, and familiar. Green lies between yellow and blue in the color spectrum; it is the foliage between the sun and sky, and its versatility is unmatched. Acting as a warm tone when weighted toward yellow, it may also serve as a cool tone when more blue is present.

We associate green with youth, health, growth, and security. Perhaps this explains why Americans have shown a preference for green automobiles during times of economic growth, most recently demonstrated in the 1990s. In interior design green is the epitome of a natural neutral. It "goes with" all other colors, and is especially effective in pulling together complex color palettes. In combination with its complement, red, green becomes powerful and elegant. In its paler, grayer tones it is soft and restful, while a lime green hue is zesty and exhilarating.

Some form of green has appeared in nearly all color palettes since the time of the Egyptians, with the celadon greens of Chinese porcelain from the Sung dynasty (A.D. 960–1276) and the subtle greens from the eighteenth-century English architects Robert and James Adams being particularly noteworthy. The soft greens of the thirteenth-century Aubusson tapestries from Flanders have also had a marked influence on interior color palettes. ▪

Subtle contrast is achieved with two different intensities, a clear, bright green silk patterned and trimmed with gold and a mellow yellow-green wall and drapery hue. Subtle white accents in shades, flowers, and candles balance a color that is both elegant and comforting. Design: Anthony Antine

Design, previous pages (from left to right): John Staff, Patricia Bonis, Anthony Antine
Design, opposite: John Staff

Right: Soft, rejuvenating green is appropriate for a living room and adjacent dining area, as well as a bedroom retreat, all with big windows for natural light. Design: Allison A. Holland

Opposite: An appetizing combination of nature's leaf green and white is a simple solution which pleases many personal tastes. Green is a very popular color for many areas of the home. Design: Barbara Eberlein

Below: A bedroom in quiet green is rejuvenating in the light of day and restful when the sun goes down. This is a complementary, contrasting color plan that bridges the need for comfort as well as for stimulation. Design: Susie Leader

Opposite: Luxuriant leaf green brings the fresh bright mood of spring to this urban window view. The background hue has been tinted to highlight the architectural trim. Design: Ronald Bricke

Left, Below: A bright kelly green with pure white sheer fabric to let all the natural light inside will lift spirits in this unique informal room. Trompe l'oeil accents add great charm and interest. Design: Anne Tarasoff

Left: Many homeowners are most comfortable with a versatile green hue. Widely used in traditional settings with sparkling white woodwork, green provides an elegant and serene background for the sparkle of lavish table settings. Design: Susie Leader

Opposite: Dark green walls with fresh white woodwork create a mood of relaxed elegance in this room furnished in the style of the great manor houses and castles of Georgian Ireland. The room is warmed by exquisite wood finishes and a sumptuous red patterned rug. Design: Paula Fogarty

Below: A versatile color that can be used in virtually every room, green is a good basis for a total color plan. Design: Allison A. Holland

Opposite: This rich green wall color is appropriate for a game room that must be refined without excess formality, matching the billiard table felt surface. White woodwork and a few brass highlights added to this relaxing green hue comprise an easy recipe for comforting color. Design: Barbara Eberlein

Right: This kitchen alcove is luxurious with architectural detail and rich color. The color tints are all in a similar range, even though the hues cover a wide spectrum. Design: Barbara Eberlein

"I typically do not use any type of color scheme repeatedly. I feel a good designer is an eclectic Dustin Hoffman, not a typical John Wayne," quips designer Al Dickerson. *"The designer will 'read and script' by establishing the proposed function of the space and then determining the color requirements of the project to best fit these objectives."*

Orange Rooms

MIDWAY BETWEEN RED AND YELLOW on the color wheel, orange is known as a color of fusion, combining two intense colors into a beautiful glowing hue which is associated with a wide variety of fruits and vegetables: oranges, of course, but also mangoes, peaches, melons, tangerines, apricots, pumpkins, and squash. Its symbolic connotation is fertility and fruition.

An attention-getting color, orange is used for warning signs and safety devices. It is also widely used for athletic clothing because it can be seen from a distance.

The mood of orange is changeable. Deep tones of orange, such as rich iron and coppery earth colors, evoke warmth and security. Pale tints of orange, like apricot and peach, are popular interior colors because they flatter all skin tones and suggest softness and delicacy. Pure orange conveys excitement and activity.

In modern interior design orange has enjoyed consistent popularity. From the Art Deco period through postmodernism, orange appears on color palettes in some form. Sometimes the tone is brilliant, sometimes burnt, sometimes peachy; orange is always warm and positive. ▪

Vivid orange upholstery brightens a conversation area and harmonizes comfortably with the natural wood ceiling and furniture pieces. Design: Steven M. Hefner; opposite: Patricia Bonis

Above: "Russet" is the name given the color in this room, another tint of orange which is subtle and comforting. The color of the walls is imbued in grass cloth, which adds texture and avoids the harsh reflections which might intensify a hue. Design: Al Dickerson

Opposite Left: Earthy burnt-orange tiles combine with gleaming white fixtures for a naturally elegant style in a bathroom. Tones of orange are favored in bathrooms because they flatter all skin tones. Design: Gail Shields-Miller

Opposite Right: Orange chair upholstery adds warmth to a contemporary breakfast area in a stylish black and white kitchen. Design: John Berenson

Opposite and below left: This dining room features deep red-orange walls with crisp white woodwork as a remarkably complementary background for exquisite linen and china and a multicolor floral arrangement. Considering the effect of color on favorite heirlooms is an important step in planning color schemes. Design: James R. Irving

Right: In this room the deep orange background of a classic rug and accent pillows in similar tones warms up cool white upholstery and walls to create a pleasing conversation area. Design: Justine Ringlien

Below right: Elegant dark wood paneling and furnishings are brightened and lightened with vivid red-orange fabrics for a mood of cheerful comfort in a library. Design: Ronald Bricke

Opposite top left and right: Deep red-orange tones of mahogany paneling surround an entertainment center and define a feeling of pleasure and relaxation. Upholstery in subtle natural tones and textures along with facing walls in warm white extend the feeling of comfort and hospitality. Design: John Berenson

Opposite bottom: A warm retreat features deep tones of rich damask fabrics against garnet walls with warm wood tones, book bindings, and flowers, completing an analogous color scheme. Design: Ho Sang Shin

Above: Peach, a delicate tint of orange, acts as a neutral backdrop for an eclectic collection of furnishings and a subdued palette of rich fabrics. Design: Gail Shields-Miller

Violet Rooms

OF ALL THE COLORS violet is the most mysteriously romantic, sending contrasting emotional messages. Its name is derived from the flower of the genus *Viola*, and particularly the fragrant *Viola odorata*, a cherished favorite for springtime nosegays. Its paler tints are delicate and fragile, connoting traditional feminine allure.

However, deep purple or violet is associated with royalty and tragedy, and its message is honor or mourning, connoting power and emotional strength.

Violet often appears in pleasing combination with its complement yellow. Deep red-violet or aubergine is a rich sophisticated color often selected by designers in lieu of black or navy, and gauzy pale lilac offers cool soft comfort in a less conventional palette.

Violet was favored in the Gay Nineties and in the grayed colored schemes popular in the 1980s. Soft tints of violet have gained popularity in the 1990s, especially in combination with yellow-greens, and recently royal purple in rich fabrics has enjoyed a comeback. ■

Violet solids and patterns in a pink "tented" room create a cozy romantic space. Design: Susie Leader; opposite: Gail Shields-Miller

Opposite: A violet rug defines a conversation area and enlivens a neutral room with much natural light. Small amounts of beautiful color give personality to a simple space. Design: Gayle Reynolds

Left: A complex color scheme is expanded from a patterned wallpaper. Painted walls and upholstery fabrics in an adjacent room echo the violet, red, and green hues in brighter tones. Design: Allison Holland

Opposite: Medium tints of pink, blue, lavender, and green create an atmosphere of soft fantasy in this child's room. An appealingly patterned green carpet ties the multi-colored palette together. Design: Lise Lawson

Right: A blue-violet carpet and deeper walls set the enchanting mood of a dining room. Bright white woodwork provides contrast and multiple windows admit natural light to clearly display the lovely colors. Design: Susie Leader

Below: A home office featuring a wall display of a doll collection is a very personal space, one where a romantic medium tint of the color violet is most appropriate. Design: Ellen Lemer Korney

Barbara Eberlein of Eberlein Design Consultants, Ltd. says "[A] sapphire dining room is a dramatic reversal from the commonly requested warm tones and immediately sets the tone for formal entertaining." She also notes that "Crisp, cool periwinkle evokes the color of the sky, on special mornings at dawn for [an] oceanside room."

CHAPTER SIX

Designers' Preferences for Individual Rooms

———◆◆◆———

As lifestyles change in contemporary society, new demands are made on many areas of the home. Kitchens have become the most heavily used family nexus, bathrooms are showrooms, bedrooms are rejuvenation stations, and living-dining areas are multi-use technological work/study and entertainment complexes. These diverse functions determine the mood needed in each space, a need which may be successfully fulfilled by careful orchestration of color palettes.

In a survey of seventy-two designers from across the United States we asked what colors they favored for specific rooms in the home. Their answers provide a guide to developing personal palettes which satisfy the comfort needs of each individual in an original way.

Living Rooms

RESEARCH INDICATES that there are certain segments of our population that entertain more than other segments; their decorating priorities reflect an interest in hospitality. Furnishings are more elaborate and decorating is more carefully planned in homes that are frequently opened to groups of friends and colleagues. A neutral palette is a "safe choice" that will satisfy nearly everyone and may also be a good backdrop for collections and fabrics of more interesting colors and textures to truly delight the eye. The number one color preferred for living rooms by the designers we surveyed is a neutral, beige, or white, chosen by 33%, followed by green, chosen by 21% of the designers, and yellow, chosen by 17%. Red, peach, and blue were in the next tier of preferred colors, and pink, salmon, apricot, and platinum were mentioned as desirable by some designers. ■

Platinum 1% Salmon/Apricot 3% Pink 4% Blue 6% Peach 7% Red 8% Yellow 17% Green 21% Beige, White 33%

Design, previous pages (from left to right): Gayle Reynolds, Allison A. Holland, Ellen Lemer Korney

Design: Gayle Reynolds

According to designer Susie Leader, "People like elegance in their living room....Color creates the 'Wow!' factor."

Dining Rooms

THE DINING ROOM SEEMS TO BE AN AREA where people assert more creativity, where stimulation of appetite and conversation are important goals, and stylish flair is less risky. Colors may be taken directly from a china pattern and translated into wall and drapery colors. Designers surveyed preferred warm nighttime colors; Red was chosen by 22% of our designers as the most desirable dining room color, 15% preferred neutrals of white or beige, 13% chose green, and 10% chose peach/salmon/apricot. Gold, yellow, and rose each were selected by 6% of the designers surveyed, and navy was mentioned by 4%. Brown, aqua, and black were mentioned by 3% of the designers, and the colors turquoise, watermelon, and ochre were mentioned also. The dining room is often the jewel of the home, sparkling and shining with crystal, silver, and fine china. ■

"[I] almost always use warm colors…peach, reds, rose, browns…colors that glow under candlelight…never acid greens, blue grays, or purples," says designer Frank Pennino of Los Angeles.

Ochre 1% Watermelon 1% Turquoise 1% Black 3% Aqua 3% Brown 3% Navy 4% Rose 6% Yellow 6% Gold 6% Peach/salmon/apricot 10% Green 13% White or beige neutrals 15% Red 26% Other 21%

Design: Allison A. Holland

"Stronger, more vibrant colors to create excitement and stimulate conversation [for dining rooms]," recommends Dallas designer Cheryl Van Duyne.

Kitchens

THE KITCHEN HAS EVOLVED into a complex area of the home, as the center for family interaction, perhaps a small home office, and more often than not, entertaining. The utilitarian requirements for light, durability, and storage are fundamental; these considerations favor neutral palettes. Traditional white is currently the comeback kitchen favored by 25% of the designers surveyed, blue was favored by 14%, green by 11%, 10% liked yellow, 8% liked wood, and 7% chose white, taupe, or beige tones. Stainless steel was the choice of 6%, and black, red, and copper were also mentioned. Planning a palette is especially critical, because most surface materials are durable with permanent colors that cannot be easily changed. Like the bathroom, kitchens are moving away from a strictly sanitary look, toward more warmth and personality. ■

"I'm seeing more ochres, honeys, and creams in the kitchen. Stainless steel adds style...copper is always great," observes designer Stacey Lapuk.

Copper 1% Red 3% Black 4% Stainless steel 6% Taupe/off-white 7% Wood 8% Yellow 10% Green 11% Blue 14% White 25% Other 11%

Design, previous pages (from left to right): Susie Leader, Allison Holland,

Design: John Staff

Bedrooms

A BEDROOM IS A PERSONAL RETREAT.
Whether a luxurious master suite or a simple guest
accommodation, this room is a haven where we spend
our precious private moments, relaxing, reflecting,
recovering. More than any other space in the house, it is
essential that our bedroom color palette makes us comfortable. Tones of blue for the bedroom were selected by 23%
of the designers surveyed, and 21% favored taupe. Peach was
recommended by 13% and green, yellow, and pink each were
suggested by 10% of the designers. The purity of white was favored
by 6%, brown and red by 3%, and gold was also mentioned. ▪

---

*"What could possibly have a wider range of
personal moods than a bedroom? Bedrooms, more
than any other space in the house, must respond to
the way a person wants to feel, not just to what
they want to see, in those special moments sepa-
rating waking and sleeping," says Barbara
Eberlein, Philadelphia designer.*

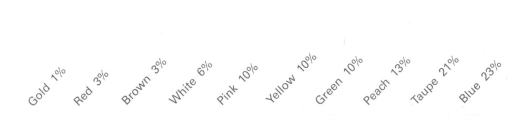

Gold 1% Red 3% Brown 3% White 6% Pink 10% Yellow 10% Green 10% Peach 13% Taupe 21% Blue 23%

Design: Ellen Lemer Korney

Bathrooms

THE INVESTMENT IN BATHROOM
FIXTURES has changed dramatically in the past
two decades, giving rise to the use of whirlpool spas,
invigorating shower appliances, and exercise equipment.
Almost every bathroom is also more lavishly decorated
than the utilitarian spaces of past generations. Luxurious
fabrics, wall coverings, accessories, and even furniture have
all made their appearance in today's baths. Off-white held the
number one spot in bath design by one percentage point with
22% of the surveyed designers recommending it, and white was
competitive with 21%. Green was favored by 7% of the surveyed designers;
black, red, and blue were mentioned by 6%, woodtones were mentioned by 4%,
peach tones by 3%, and gray, chrome, and gold each were recommended by 1%
of the designers. ■

*Barbara Eberlein explains, "Bathrooms . . . have
come a long way from the days of antiseptic white
tile and fixtures to deep rich colors and materials
which produce the feeling of a room, not just a
bathroom."*

Gold 1% Chrome 1% Gray 1% Peach 3% Wood 4% Blue 6% Red 6% Black 6% Green 7% White 21% Off-whites 22% Other 22%

Family Rooms

CONTEMPORARY HOME PLANS often combine the family room with the living room and perhaps also the dining room to create what is now known as the "great room."

But the most recent change is the addition of technology: computer workstations for adults and children, computer games, and internet stations, as well as the basic television and video viewing area are evolving. This is the room that seems to be changing fastest as we transition to the twenty-first century. It is a room that lends itself to informal and soothing earth tones, colors that also require less maintenance. Blues, greens, taupes, and beiges predominate. Green is the most popular color for family rooms among our surveyed designers, with 19% recommending it; 17% favored red for a close second, and 14% advised using earth tones. Blue was chosen by 11% of the designers, 8% favored off-whites and beiges. White and brown each received recommendations from 3% of the experts. Other colors mentioned were teal, eggplant, wood, pink, and apricot. ■

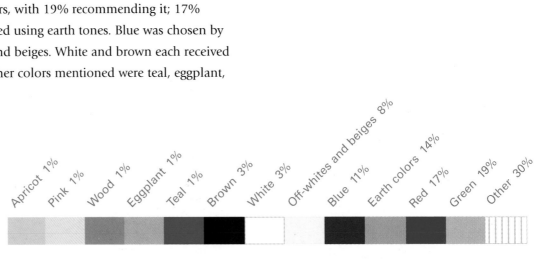

Apricot 1% Pink 1% Wood 1% Eggplant 1% Teal 1% Brown 3% White 3% Off-whites and beiges 8% Blue 11% Earth colors 14% Red 17% Green 19% Other 30%

Design: Sue Wenk

Regarding color preferences for family rooms, California designer Ellen Lemer Korney says "[I'll use] any mid-range of color that hides dirt!"

Bibliography

Anderson, Donald M. *Elements of Design.* New York: Holt, Rinehart and Winston, 1961.

Best From the Interior Design Hall of Fame. Grand Rapids, Michigan: Vitae Publishing, Inc., 1992.

Birren, Faber. *Color and Human Response,* New York: Van Nostrand Reinhold, 1978.

Birren, Faber. *Color for Interiors, Historical and Modern.* New York: Whitney Library of Design, 1963.

Chijiiwa, Hideaki. *Color Harmony.* Rockport, Massachusetts: Rockport Publishers, 1987.

Choosing a Color Scheme. Upper Saddle River, New Jersey: Creative Homeowner Press, 1992.

Color Sourcebook. Rockport, Massachusetts: Rockport Publishers, Inc., 1989.
Color Sourcebook II. Rockport, Massachusetts: Rockport Publishers, Inc., 1989.

Dondis, Donis A. *A Primer of Visual Literacy.* Cambridge, Massachusetts: The MIT Press, 1973.

Gale, Iain and Susan Irvine. *Laura Ashley Style.* New York: Harmony Books, 1987.

Hope, Augustine and Margaret Walch. *The Color Compendium.* New York, Van Nostrand Reinhold, 1990.

Innes, Jocasta. *The New Paint Magic.* New York: Pantheon Books, a division of Random House, 1992.

Kobayashi, Shigenobu. *Color Image Scale.* New York: Kodansha, Ltd.

Krippner, Stanley and Daniel Rubin, editors. *The Kirlian Aura.* New York: Anchor Books, 1974.

Ladau, Robert F. *Color in Interior Design and Architecture.* New York: Van Nostrand Reinhold.

Lüscher, Max. *The Lüscher Color Test,* translated and edited by Ian Scott. New York: Washington Square Press, 1969.

Mc Kim, Robert H. *Thinking Visually.* Palo Alto, California: Dale Seymour Publications, 1980.

Preble, Duane and Sarah. *Artforms,* Fourth Edition. New York: Harper and Row, 1989.

Sargent, Walter. *The Enjoyment and Use of Color.* New York: Dover Publications, Inc., 1964.

Showcase of Interior Design; Eastern Edition, Midwest Edition, Pacific Edition, Southern Edition. Grand Rapids, Michigan: Vitae Publishing, Inc.,1989-1993.

Snyder, David. *Epoustouflant.* Santa Monica, California: 1990.

Walch, Margaret and Augustine Hope. *Living Colors.* San Francisco: Chronicle Books, 1995.

Whelan, Bride M. *Color Harmony.* Rockport, Massachusetts: Rockport Publishing Company, 1994.

Wydra, Nancilee. *Feng Shui in the Garden.* Chicago, Illinois: Comtemporary Publishing Company, 1997.

Index of Designers

Diane Alpern Kovacs, ASID associate
Diane Alpern Kovacs Interior Design, Inc.
4 Main Street
Roslyn, NY 11576
ph. 516/625-0703
fax 516/625-8441
254 E. 68th St.
New York, NY 10021
19, 31, 39, 70

Anthony Antine
Antine Associates, Inc.
750 Park Ave.
New York, NY 10021
ph. 212/988-4096
ph. 201/224-0315
fax 201/941-9250
35, 42, 44, 85, 101, 106, 110, 111,
113, 115

Brett Beldock
Brett Design, Inc.
201 E. 87th St.
New York, NY 10128
ph. 212/987-8270
fax 212/987-8315
61, 62, 66, 74, 76, 78

John Berenson, ASID
John Berenson Interior Design
180 N.E. 39th St., Suite 220
Miami, FL 33137
ph. 305/576-6049
fax 305/576-6087
7, 103, 105, 127, 130, 149

Patricia Bonis
Patricia Bonis Interiors, Inc.
979 Third Ave., Suite 2C
New York, NY 10022
ph. 212/ 980-6040
fax 212/980-4760
22, 24, 26, 33, 41, 56, 60, 69, 109, 110, 112,
124

Ronald Bricke, honorary member ASID
Ronald Bricke & Associates, Inc.
333 E. 69th St.
New York, NY 10021
ph. 212/472-9006
fax 212/472-9008
18, 58, 64, 67, 87, 93, 94, 95, 104, 119, 129

Mary Delany
Mary Delany Interior Design
1 Strawberry Hill Ct.
Stamford, CT 06902
ph. 203/348-6839
7

Al Dickerson
Klingman's of Grand Rapids
3525 28th St. SE
Grand Rapids, MI 49512
126

Donna Dunn, ASID
Donna Dunn & Associates
41-865 Boardwalk, Suite 105
Palm Desert, CA 92211
ph. 760/340-9598
fax 760/568-1968
54, 69, 71

Barbara Eberlein
Eberlein Design Consultants, Ltd.
1809 Walnut St., Suite 101
Philadelphia, PA 19103
ph. 215/405-0400
fax 215/405-0588
28, 32, 34, 40, 45, 56, 63, 68, 91, 103, 109,
116, 122, 123

William R. Eubanks
William R. Eubanks Interior Design, Inc.
1516 Union Ave.
Memphis, TN 38104
ph. 901/272-1825
fax 901/272-1845
36

Al Evans
No address available
2, 28, 76, 80, 90

Paula Fogarty
Kindel Furniture Company
100 Garden St.
P.O. Box 2047
Grand Rapids, MI 49501
ph. 616/243-3676
fax 616/243-6248
www.kindelfurniture.com
4, 121

Gary Gibson
Gary Gibson Interior Design
511 N. La Cienega Blvd. Suite 202
Los Angeles, CA 90048
ph. 310/659-1684
fax 310/659-1881
38

Phyllis G. Goldberg, ASID
PGG Interiors
P.O. Box 14427
East Providence, RI 02914
ph. 401/331-7077
fax 401/331-7077
60

Steven M. Hefner, ASID
Designworks Creative Partnership, Ltd.
6501 Park of Commerce Blvd., #B-205
Boca Raton, FL 33487
ph. 561/912-9860
fax 561/912-9865
73, 96, 125

Allison A. Holland
Creative Decorating
168 Poloke Place
Honolulu, HI 96822
ph. 808/955-1465
fax 808/943-8450
36, 79, 81, 106, 108, 117, 120, 134,
138, 143

Nancy Craig Hollingsworth
519 Fenton Place.
Charlotte, NC 28207
ph. 704/377-3625
fax 704/374-9592
74

James R. Irving, ASID
13901 Shaker Blvd.
Cleveland, OH 44120
ph. 216/283-1991 (home office)
ph. 216/751-1100 (switchboard)
128, 129

Stacey Lapuk, ASID, CID
Stacey Lapuk Interior Design, Inc.
437 Wellesley Ave.
Mill Valley, CA 94941
ph. 415/383-9223
fax 415/381-6646
www.realestateanddesign.com/Stacey.html
43, 52, 70, 72, 73

Vince Lattuca
Visconti & Company
245 E. 57th St., 2nd Floor
New York, NY 10022
ph. 212/758-2720
fax 212/758-2731
64

Lise Lawson, ASID
Lise Lawson Interior Design
6420 N. Lake Dr.
Fox Point, WI 53217
ph. 414/351-6334
fax 414/351-4480
81, 136

Susie Leader
Susie Leader Interiors
1280 Latham
Birmingham, MI 48009
ph. 248/642-2571
fax 248/642-9897
82, 117, 120, 133, 137

Ellen Lemer Korney, ASID, CID
Ellen Lemer Korney Associates
10170 Culver Blvd.
Culver City, CA 90232
ph. 310/204-6576
fax 310/204-1457
27, 55, 86, 137, 139, 147

Lila Levinson, ASID, CKD, CID
Accent on Design
2075 De La Cruz Blvd., Ste. 101
Santa Clara, CA 95050
ph. 408/988-4600
9, 21, 47, 51, 92

Susan Lovelace, allied member ASID
Lovelace Interiors
12870 U.S. 98 West
Destin, FL 32541
ph. 850/837-5563
fax 850/654-5867
66

Sandra Nunnerley
Sandra Nunnerley, Inc.
575 Madison Ave.
New York, NY 10022
ph. 212/472-9341
fax 212/472-9346
8, 12, 16, 22, 23, 30, 34, 37, 39, 75

Gayle Reynolds, ASID, IIDA
Gayle Reynolds Design
7 Fessenden Way
Lexington, MA 02173
ph. 781/863-5169
fax 781/863-1104
6, 47, 53, 55, 65, 135, 138, 141

Justine Ringlien, ASID
96 Ridgeview Dr.
Atherton, CA 94027
ph. 650/233-0330
fax 650/854-7733
8, 11, 58, 71, 84, 129

Lynn Robinson, allied member ASID
Lynn Robinson Interiors
Powers Bldg.
34 Audry Ave.
Oyster Bay, NY 11771
ph. 516/921-4455
89

Pedro Rodriguez, FASID
Pedro Rodriguez Interiors
2215 Locust St.
Philadelphia, PA 19103
ph. 215/561-3884
fax 215/561-3884
49, 84

David A. Seglin, AIA
HSP/Ltd., Seglin Associates
430 W. Erie, #510
Chicago, IL 60610
ph. 312/573-1300
fax 312/573-0866
14

Gail Shields-Miller
Shields & Company Interiors
149 Madison Ave., Suite 201
New York, NY 10016
ph. 212/679-9130
fax 212/679-9140
15, 20, 31, 127, 131, 132

Ho Sang Shin
Antine Associates, Inc.
750 Park Ave.
New York, NY 10021
ph. 212/988-4096
ph. 212/224-0315
fax 212/941-9250
17, 40, 107, 130

John Staff
J. Staff Architect
2148-C Federal Ave.
Los Angeles, CA 90025
ph. 310/477-9972
fax 310/477-0535
16, 77, 100, 112, 114, 145

Pat Stotler, allied member ASID
Pat Stotler Interiors
7650 E. Williams Dr. #1060
Scottsdale, AZ 85255
ph. 602/342-8038
fax 602/342-8072
13

Anne Tarasoff
Anne Tarasoff Interiors
25 Andover Rd.
Port Washington, NY 11050
ph. 516/944-8913
fax 516/944-7256
46, 98, 99, 118

Sanford R. Thigpen
Sanford R. Thigpen Interiors, Inc.
2996 Grandview Ave., N.E., Ste. 310
Atlanta, GA 30305
ph. 404/351-1411
fax 404/240-0558
33, 102

Jean Valente
Jean Valente, Inc.
175 E. 79th St.
New York, NY 10021
ph. 212/472-4574
fax 212/472-2221
59, 96

Jill Vantosh, ISSD
Vantosh & Associates
1477 Spring St.
Atlanta, GA 30309
ph. 404/888-0613
fax 404/876-0191
42, 48

Stephanie Walters, IIDA, CCIDC
Parisi Interior Design
2002 Jimmy Durante Blvd., #308
Del Mar, CA 92014
ph. 619/259-0031
50, 57

Carole Weaks, IIDA
C. Weaks Interiors, Inc.
3391 Habersham Rd.
Atlanta, GA 30305
ph. 404/233-6040
fax 404/233-6043
51

Sue Wenk
Sue Wenk Interior Design
300 E. 71st St.
New York, NY 10021
ph. 212/879-5149
29, 83, 88, 97, 151

Index of Photographers

Dennis Anderson
No address available
8, 11, 58, 84

Alexander Anton
Alexander Anton/Studio 53
53 N. Main St.
Atlantic City, NJ 08232
ph. 609/641-2934
fax 609/641-2772
49, 84

Jamie Ardiles-Arce
730 5th Ave.
New York, NY 10019
ph. 212/333-8779
8, 16, 22, 23, 30, 34, 37, 39, 75

John Canham
Quadra Focus Photography
588 Waite Ave.
Sunnyvale, CA 94086
ph. 408/739-1465
fax 408/739-9117
9, 21, 47, 51, 92

Judith Carlson
Judith Carlson Photography
31 Glen Way
Cold Spring Harbor, NY 11724
ph. 516/692-5215
89

Arthur Coleman
Coleman Photography
303 N. Indian Canyon Dr.
Palm Springs, CA 92262
ph. 760/325-7015
fax 760/320-6066
www.arthurcoleman.com
71

Chris Corrie
Chris Corrie Photography
981 Calle Carmilita
Santa Fe, NM 87501
ph., fax 505/473-4178
7, 38

Tom Crane
Tom Crane Photography, Inc.
113 Cumberland Place
Bryn Mawr, PA 19010
ph. 610/525-2444
28, 32, 34, 40, 45, 56, 63, 68, 76, 78, 91,
103, 109, 116, 122, 123

Al Dickerson
Klingman's of Grand Rapids
3525 28th St. SE
Grand Rapids, MI 49512
126

Phillip Ennis
Phillip Ennis Photography
114 Millertown Rd.
Bedford, NY 10506
ph. 914/234-9574
fax 914/234-0360
www.phillip-ennis.com
110

Feliciano
480 Broadway, Suite 302
New York, NY 10013
12

Eric Figge
No address available
50

Dan Forer
6815 SW 81st Terrace
Miami, FL 33143
ph. 305/667-3646
fax 305/667-4733
28, 76, 80, 90, 125

Scott Frances
No address available
61, 62, 66, 76, 78

Jack Gardner
Jack Gardner Photography
P.O. Box 7
Valparaiso, FL
ph. 850/678-7702
fax 850/729-1331
66

Michael E. Garland
No address available
137

Brian Gassel
1719 Briarlake Cr.
Decatur, GA 30033
ph. 404/315-8655
42, 48

Arthur M. Gray
171 Pier Ave., #272
Santa Monica, CA 90405
ph. 310/450-2806
fax 310/392-7550
77, 100, 112, 114, 145

Sam Gray
374 Congress St.
Boston, MA 02210
ph. 781/237-2711
fax 617/482-1844
sgp@samgray.com
55

Michael Hill
333 E. 69th St.
New York, NY 10021
ph. 212/472-9006
fax 212/472-9008
18, 58, 64, 67, 87, 93, 94, 95, 104, 119, 129

Roger Hill
Studio 139
139 Grandville S.W.
Grand Rapids, MI 49503
ph. 616/235-4455
4, 121

Michael Hunter
No address available
46

Peter Jaquith
Peter Jaquith Photography
6 Pleasant St.
Beverly, MA 01915
ph. 508/921-4737
60

John Jensen
1421 Castro St.
San Francisco, CA 94114
ph. 516/676-2726
23, 37

Ethan Kaminsky
Kaminsky Productions
870 Research Dr., Ste. 10
Palm Springs, CA 92262
ph. 760/323-8392
fax 760-864-1657
www.kaminskyproductions.com
54, 69

Tom Knibbs
No address available
96

Paul Kopelow
147 West 25th St.
New York, NY 10001
ph. 212/929-2686
fax 212/929-2582
19, 31, 39, 70

Tim Lee
Tim Lee Photography
2 Zachary Ln.
New Milford, CT 06776
ph. 860/355-4661
fax 860/350-3526
17, 40, 42, 44, 106, 107, 113, 115, 130

David Duncan Livingston
1036 Erica Road
Mill Valley, CA 94941
www.davidduncanlivingston.com
27, 36, 79, 81, 108, 117, 120, 138, 143

Salvatore M. Lovinello
Salvatore M. Lovinello Photography
610 Chestnut Blvd.
Chesterton, IN 46304
ph. 219/395-9016
fax 219/395-8020
14

Beth Singer
Beth Singer, Photographer
25741 River Rd.
Franklin, MI 48025
ph. 248/626-4860
82, 117, 120, 133, 137

John Sutton
John Sutton Architectural Photography
8 Main St.
Point San Quentin, CA 94964
ph. 415/258-8100
fax 415/258-8167
43, 52, 70, 72, 73

Bill Timmerman
382 N. First Ave.
Phoenix, AZ 85003
ph. 602/420-9325
fax 602/420-9326
57

Jeanne Van Atta
Green Street Studio
3637 S. Green Rd., Suite 3D
Beachwood, OH 44122
ph. 216/464-1997
fax 216/292-7796
128, 129

Eric A. Zepeda
1451 Stevenson St.
Studio A
San Francisco, CA 94103
ph. 415/558-9691
71, 129

About the Authors

JOHN AND MELANIE AVES met in their art and
English classes at Albion College in Michigan, a forecast of the
three decades they have spent together exploring design, litera-
ture, and education. Melanie has been associated with various
schools and universities as teacher, professor, and a lifelong
student in the field of art and journalism. John consults with
several home furnishings companies on marketing and design
development. They have been involved with the publication of
over 20 books on interior design, many of which have been
translated into several languages and are sold throughout the
world. The Aves have three daughters and live in a restored
110-year-old French Victorian style cottage overlooking Macatawa
Bay in western Michigan. ▨